Dedication and Acknowledgements

I dedicate this book to the loving memory of my mother Josephine B. Malachi for it is because of her that I am the person many of you know today. My mother gave me so much. She left a rich legacy, which included what it means to be a strong, beautiful, fashion sense, money wise, empowered, faithful and spiritual wife, mother, sister, and aunt.

I especially want to thank my father Leroy Malachi for always encouraging me (and my brothers) to succeed in life to always be in control and responsible for my decisions and actions. When things did not always go the way we wanted them to or we made mistakes-- he would tell us to accept the outcome as one of life's lessons, learn from the experience, and move forward.

There are so many more people who helped make my book a reality, but the numbers are too many to mention them all.

However, I must acknowledge and thank some people because, without their constant urging to write this book–, it would have never happened. My son's Marshall IV and Christopher, I love you and thank you so much for your love and being there for me whenever I needed you; Letitia Shelby for always saying "You should write a book about shopping" every time when I shared my shopping adventures with her and our other friends.

Finally, but of course not all, I want to thank my granddaughter Rikara for taking the photos of my closets and drawers that are provided as examples of how to get organized; and to Joyce Young, for taking the time to edit the first of many versions of this book before it was published.

Sincere and special thanks to my husband of 39 years, Marshall III, for supporting my dreams, passions and providing me with loving and constructive criticism during the writing this book.

How I shop is not a big mystery.

Dedication and Acknowledgements

We all have heard some or all of these principles mentioned in this book at one time or another. However, hearing and follow through with doing does require discipline and self-control.

I believe that shoppers need to understand and believe that they are ultimately the only one responsible for their decisions as to where, what and when they spend their money.

Therefore, it is my opinion that if you allow these shopping principles to become a continuous part of your shopping routine, they will help you towards complete mastery to becoming the empowered shopper I know you can be!

Shopping; Shopping; Shopping; Shopping;

Shopping

Shopping With

ESP

Essential Shopping Principles
An easy-to-use book to becoming an
Empowered Shopper

Shopping With ESP

Essential Shopping Principles

A Pat's Closet Publication
San Ramon, California 94583

<u>Disclaimer</u>

The author/publisher of the book does not guarantee that you will be cured from any compulsive shopping behavior or habits. The author/publisher makes no warranties with respect to the content of this book and shall in no event be held liable for any loss or other damages, including but not limited to special incidental consequences, or damages. As always, the advice of a therapist or medical professional for compulsive behavior should be sought.

First Edition

Library of Congress Cataloging-in-Publication Data
Shopping with ESP/Patricia Lott
p. cm.
Includes index.

ISBN 0615285732
ISBN 978-0-615-28573-3

Shopping With

ESP

Essential Shopping Principles

Table of Contents

Introduction

"Education remains the key to both economic and political empowerment". Barbara Jordan, 1991

The next time you go shopping
Take along your

Essential Shopping Principles

I love to shop and for as long as I can remember shopping has always been a wonderful and fun experience. My mother was a great shopper, and she was one of those shoppers who would buy something, put it in the closet (with the tags) and then give it away because she had forgot about it and then realize she would never wear it. Her closets were always neat and organized everything in its place, dresses, blouses, skirts, arranged by color and length and the matching purses and hats on the closet shelf. She had her closet and my dad had his.

Now that I am an adult, I realize that so much of what I enjoy about shopping came solely from my mother. I can enjoy shopping every day and I do not have to buy a single thing. I know what I want or need and better than that, I know what I already have and what needs to be replaced or accessorized.

I was a military wife for twenty-seven years, which forced me to discard things I did not need or no longer wanted every time we moved. My husband was an officer in the United States Coast Guard and he was often transferred to a new assignment that sometimes required us to move every four years. It was during these times that I would take the opportunity to clean out my closets and draws and give away things that I no longer needed or wanted.

My rule was --- if I had not worn or used something by the time of our move – then I did not need it.

Get Rid of the Clutter

Shopping With

ESP

Essential Shopping Principles

Today, now that my husband has retired from active service, I do the same, but I have shortened the timeframe: If I have not used or worn something in two years – then it is time to give it away. This helps me to eliminate the clutter and make room for something new.

Therefore, I have decided to share my philosophy and shopping habits with you – in hope that you will find the same enjoyment that I have and that this book will inspire you to become a wiser and empowered shopper by developing and mastering ESP!

This is your ultimate book for a great, empowering, and fun shopping experience every time you spend your money. It is my wish that you will want to share this book with everyone you know. It will not matter whether the person is male or female – It is my belief that we all need to be better stewards of our money in order to be empowered.

The book is easy to follow and promises to provide you with the knowledge and information you can rely on, to enjoy years of empowering shopping.

Shopping With

ESP

Essential Shopping Principles

So, before you buy another dress, pair of shoes, piece of jewelry or any other wardrobe accessory—please follow my advice and recommendations for becoming a very wise, experienced and happy Shopper!!!!

I dedicate this book to the memory of my mother and all of her fine qualities that have contributed to making me the wise shopper I am today and so much more.

My belief and philosophy is that there are just seven essential shopping principles. These principles, in my opinion, will help make your shopping experience one of sheer pleasure, delight, and fun.

I believe that knowing and carrying out these principles will give you the economic freedom and empowerment to choose when and where you spend your money.

Once you learn and adapt these principles to your life you will truly enjoy and understand the meaning of "Shop till you Drop" every time you go shopping.

Shopping With

ESP

Essential Shopping Principles

The 7 Essential Shopping Principles

1. Make an Attitude Adjustment
2. Inventory and Be Familiar with What You Have
3. Eliminate: Clear out the Clutter and Get Organized
4. Shop with Patience
5. Window Shop
6. Purchase What You Need First and What You Want Last
7. Enjoy Yourself and Have Fun

Shopping With

Essential Shopping Principles

How many times have you heard the saying Patience is a virtue?

Well, I am a firm believer in this saying. Having patience is the first principle and the fundamental foundation for becoming a smart and expert shopper.

Shopping with Patience is the ultimate key to your successful shopping experience, so make sure you allow yourself ample time to shop whenever you have the need or want to go shopping.

How many times do you find yourself buying in a hurry? The time you have allotted yourself is unrealistic, but you make the purchase anyhow.

Unfortunately, you seem to know immediately after leaving the store that you have not made a sensible or reasonable purchase.

For example, you have a special occasion and you decide on the day of the event that you want something new to wear.

Shopping With

ESP

Essential Shopping Principles

It does not matter that you have known about this event for several weeks or even months; and that you have several closets full of special occasion outfits to choose. However, for you, the urgency is now!

You have convinced yourself that nothing in your closet is good enough to wear to the event.

You have come to this conclusion through a process only known to those individuals who have mastered the art of rationale and impulse buying.

Therefore, you drive out to the nearest mall or boutique to find and buy something to wear (with less than an hour to spare before the event).

You do this knowing that the purchase will be costly (even if you convince yourself you have gotten a deal on your purchase) and one that you will
question yourself about later. “Why did I buy this outfit and what was I thinking”?

Another example of shopping without patience is that you are just feeling unhappy, depressed, or just want to spend money (this situation can apply to both men and women) so you decide that you just want a Shopping Fix to cure this ill.

You need it now and have very little time to make a "Sensible or Reasonable Purchase".

If at any time you have experienced anything like these examples, then you have given up your ability to be financially empowered. You have released
and given permission to the retailer to spend your money as they think you should.

You are allowing yourself to be pressured to buy the first outfit the salesperson says looks good on you. You so graciously respond with the words they want to hear – "Really, I'll take it."

Time has just become the controlling force that ignites and fuels your desire to make that purchase. This has to be the case, because what other excuse is there for not making a "Sensible or Reasonable Purchase".

Shopping With

Essential Shopping Principles

Ladies (or Gentlemen) shopping for that outfit on the same day of your special occasion or because you need a "Shopping Fix" to make you feel better ultimately leads to a closet full of Nothing to Wear. So, if any one of these scenarios sounds familiar:

Red Light — Stop — Put on The Brakes— Quick!

From this moment forward it's time for you to change gears, take hold and take charge of yourself, and make an "Attitude Adjustment" about your "Shopping Habits" and "Shopping Purchases."

Shopping With

ESP

Essential Shopping Principles

No longer will you have to feel guilty about a purchase and no longer will you need to question yourself about a ridiculous purchase you may have made.

The Ideal and Most Empowering Way to Shop!

Shopping With

ESP

Essential Shopping Principles

Shopping Principle One
"Make an Attitude Adjustment"

Making an "Attitude Adjustment" about your shopping habits will not happen overnight (remember you are trying to change shopping behavior that has taken years to develop).

Like anything new, it will take several tries until you have mastered and can realize the change within yourself.

You can begin your "Attitude Adjustment" journey to complete mastery by following this recommended "Attitude Adjustment Roadmap":

1. Shut out the Music in your head that sings the old, too familiar song "Let's Go Shopping – A Shopping I must go" when you have a limited amount of time to shop (limited time = you have less than 2 hours to spare).

This is when most shoppers get into trouble. They are rushed and they feel pressured to buy something. Often times you convince yourself that you have found or made the purchase of a lifetime.

Yes, this can happen with a little luck, but it will not happen every time you shop with a limited amount of time.

It is my belief that real bargains and true savings are realized when you have time to leisurely go through a store. This way you can look at displays, go through the many clothing or shoe racks of sale and non-sale items.

When you have time to do this you can really assess if there is an opportunity to save money or just compare prices.

There is no real pressure or time constraints and you get to just "Fondle the items" (as my dear shopping partner likes to say) and to place selective items on what I like to refer to as "**My Shoppers' Watch Alert**" (waiting for the "right price" that I am willing to pay). Step back, take a deep breath and clear your mind in order to take charge of yourself and the on-coming symptoms of the "Shopper's Fever" that comes over you suddenly; like the flu.

This is when you have a burning desire to spend money and have no idea what you need. You just want to buy something. This is a great opportunity to go:

"Window Shopping" (I will explain this later).

Sometimes the urge will be too great to ignore and you find yourself at the mall, specialty store, or boutique. Therefore, when this happens --- one exercise you may want to practice is this.

Take the **"Validity Self Check Test"** (for spending your money). Ask yourself the following question:

Is this something I need or is this something I want?

You must be truthful with yourself in order for this "Validity Self Check Test" to work.

You will know the test is working when you can respond with confidence and certainty with either: Need or Want.

Here is an example to assist you with this concept:

You are in the shoe department at Nordstrom's and find that they are having a 40% sale on women designer shoes with an additional 30% off the sale price.

Very Tempting, Right?

Shopping With

ESP

Essential Shopping Principles

You try on a pair of classy and sexy bronze color heels.

You tell yourself that these shoes will go perfectly with an outfit you purchased a week ago. Even though the shoes look great on your feet, you exercise the “Validity Self Check Test”.

Do I need these shoes? On the other hand, do I want these shoes?

Before responding, you take a quick mental assessment of your current shoe inventory and realize that you already have 2 pairs of classy and sexy bronze heels that will go perfectly with your new outfit.

Therefore, you response: “I want these shoes”

Therefore, it is now easier for you to leave them on the rack and just “Window Shop”

Shopping With

Essential Shopping Principles

I know I am making this sound way too simple and easy, and I know that some of you will need to make a huge paradigm shift from your normal behavior and shopping habits.

Ultimately, you alone decide what goes into the shopping cart!

Men, I am sure you have had the same experience and this exercise will work for you as well.

Do not expect to succeed at this technique the first time you try it. You must keep trying and strive to make achievement of this technique a personal goal.

Once you have mastered this technique, get ready for many unique and empowering shopping experiences.

In my opinion this is also an exercise towards one's "Financial Empowerment". You will be empowered to spend your money when you are ready not because the store has a sale on shoes or anything else.

2. Avoid shopping in a "Delirious State of Mind" causing you to question afterwards why you even made the purchases you did (Losing your Financial Empowerment)

Shopping With

ESP

Essential Shopping Principles

It is too easy to make excuses to justify unnecessary spending, such as:

- Just got a raise or a bonus
- Just got paid and it's the weekend
- Received a tax refund check
- Want to have a Pity Party where you are the guest of honor

Unconsciously you spend yours or someone else's hard earned money with no regard or thought about what you are buying.

You are in the moment, a negative state of being, or in a state of 'Funk" and you believe the only cure is to go shopping. Somehow, this negative state of being is not a major concern (until after the credit card bill arrives or you decide to balance your checkbook).

Guess what?

The fix is only temporary and you are still not satisfied because you have spent money while in a "Delirious State of Mind".

Shopping With

Essential Shopping Principles

Finally!

3. Set aside adequate time to shop in order to make a complete and thorough sweep of a store.

For example, when shopping in a store the size of:

- Marshall's you should allow yourself at least 1 hour
- A small clothing boutique or consignment store you need 30 minutes to 1 hour
- Mall shopping you should allow yourself at least 2 hours (minimally).

Personally, I like to set aside a whole morning or afternoon to shop at the mall. I can easily spend as much as 2 hours in Nordstrom's alone.

Shopping With

Essential Shopping Principles

Once you have achieved mastery of your "Attitude Adjustment", you will be ready to exercise and experience the ultimate and wonderful shopping experience of a person who is in control and financially empowered.

Smart Shoppers are Empowered

Shopping With

ESP

Essential Shopping Principles

Shopping Principle Two
"Inventory and be Familiar with what you Have"

How many of you can honestly say that you know exactly every piece of clothing you have in your closet or closets; and all of the accessories you own?

I would guess that the number of you who do would be small compared to the number of you who do not have a clue.

For as long as I can remember, I have practiced the habit of doing a rotating inventory of my belongings. It started out as a chore that my mother would have me do just before the changing of each season.

The first time that she actually had me do this on my own, I was in junior high school. I had my own bedroom, being the only girl of four children, and in my room, I had 2 built-in closets, 1 standalone closet and a large size dresser with four drawers.

Shopping With

Essential Shopping Principles

My mother would have my clothes separated into different categories, which included:

- Church Clothes & Shoes
- School Clothes & Shoes
- After School Cloths & Shoes
- Hats and Handbags and other accessories

At the beginning of each season (winter, spring, summer, and fall). I would go through my closets and drawers; and take an inventory of what I had.

I would try on last year's clothing to see if they still fit and tell my mother so that she would know what she needed to buy me for each season. Being the only girl in the house was great because that meant I would be getting new clothes once I out grew what I had and I did not have a sister to share my things.

As an adult, I find that my inventory frequency occurs monthly, however, the process in slightly different -- one month I will inventory my closets (Clothes and Shoes), next month my drawers, next my jewelry, then my hats and other accessories.

The nice thing about this process is that I become familiar with what I have and it also allows me to see how I might mix and match different pieces.

The key to mastering this process is realized once you are able to go shopping and have the ability to make a purchase with a recall of what you currently have in your closets or drawers.

For example, I was shopping in Chico's where I had purchased a 2-piece navy blue pants outfit 2 years ago.

I saw a multi-color sweater that would go perfect with the outfit I owned. As I continued to think about what I owned I knew that I also have a hat that has the same colors as the sweater.

Being familiar with my inventory helped me with making the decision to make the purchase. I made the old outfit new just by adding a new accessory.

The other nice thing about doing an ongoing inventory of what you own is that you can no longer say you have nothing to wear and you have to be completely honest with yourself.

The inventory also becomes a reality check as to how much you really do have and assists you with being honest when you do the Validity Self Check Test.

I know that you are wondering when you will ever have the time to do an inventory of your closets, drawers, or even a storage unit (additional storage required because you have run out of space in your home or apartment).

Nevertheless, believe me you will want to make time and once you do – you will ask yourself why you waited so long to begin this process.

I find that when I am bored and think that I might want to go shopping that this is the perfect time for me to do an inventory. I begin the process and before you know it, I am no longer bored and I am deep into what I have started to the point that I do not want to stop until I am finished.

Shopping With

ESP

Essential Shopping Principles

This can be an overwhelming process for some, especially if you have several closets full of clothes. Therefore, I would suggest that you start small. Take on one area every quarter until you have completed one full cycle. A cycle is a year and it would include clothes, shoes, accessories, lingerie, and jewelry.

Of course, once you have mastered this process, you may find that there are other categories you may want to add. The idea is to complete this process every three months or as frequently as you see fit.
Here is an example of my personal inventory cycle:

1st Quarter: Clothes (including eveningwear)

2nd Quarter: Accessories (hats, scarves, shoes)

3rd Quarter: Jewelry (fashion, fine and watches)

4th Quarter: Lingerie

The routine is an easy process to follow and maintain:

- Take an inventory of your closets, drawers, storage unit, and any other place you may have your belongings stored.
- Get familiar with your belongings so that you will really know what you have. You will soon be very familiar with

the styles, colors, quantities, and sizes you own. I like to begin the year by doing an inventory of my clothes and I like to separate them by seasons. I usually have the current season's clothes in my main closet and store the other seasons' clothing in another closet. By doing my inventory at the beginning of the year I am familiar with what I already own and have an idea of what is needed (if anything) for that season.

The other nice thing about this process is that I get "me time" and I just have a ball going through my stuff and putting my closet and drawers in order. My husband knows when he does not see me for a couple of hours that I am upstairs going through my clothing and accessories.

Try it and you will be amazed at how much you will gain from this experience. You will be able to have a mental picture in your mind as to what you have and what you will need to add as an accessory to complement any outfit you already own.

For many this principle will take months to complete so do not get frustrated, discourage, or give up. There will be a point when you may feel over whelmed, but remember you have been shopping for years….

This leads me to the next and very important principle; which goes hand and hand with this one.

The next principle will be very painful for some, especially those of you who keep everything whether you can wear it or not.

You have convinced yourself that there is a good reason for keeping those things around, but in all honesty, you do not even know you have them until you accidentally come across them when you are looking for something else. So read on and learn about principle number three.

Shopping With

Essential Shopping Principles

When you have everything in its place – accessorizing is much easier to do!

Shopping With

Essential Shopping Principles

Shopping Principle Three
"Eliminate, Clear Out the Clutter and Get Organized"

This is probably the hardest principle to accept and master for most of us. Believe me it was hard for me at first, but I learned quickly to embrace and continue this practice.

I mentioned earlier that I contribute my success to years of conditioning in my youth and being married to a person in the United States Coast Guard. Therefore, I know firsthand how to get organized.

Eliminating or getting rid of personal belongings carries with it all sorts of reasons for wanting to do just the opposite – hold on. It is so much easier for us to keep things no matter how long we have had them or how old they are even when there just is not any room to store another thing in our closets or drawers.

Sure, we convince ourselves that fashions do come around again and that something will always be in style. Okay – let us be realistic – fashions do repeat themselves, but guess what- they are not identical to the style that was before and the fabric is usually different from the original fabric.

I have family members and friends who are somewhat sentimental and they love vintage and period pieces. Many of whom believe that holding on to certain items and pieces of clothing is a good thing, because they believe these items to be fashionable and timeless (your classic piece, never to go out of style).

Okay, news flash --- the reality is this—clothing, even if you think they are timeless, ask yourself this question – "What is the chance that you will even consider or even be able to wear them again"? Now jewelry and other accessories may be different. You will probably have a greater chance to continue to wear these items, so in my opinion these are truly timeless items.

There are other items that I would consider keeping, like purses, jewelry, scarves, and sweaters.

However, even these items needed to be evaluated and examined to make sure they are in a condition worth hanging on to.

When you are going through the process of doing an inventory and becoming familiar with your belongings, you will also have to force yourself to "Eliminate".

Shopping With

ESP

Essential Shopping Principles

If this closet looks anything like yours then you are going to want to …

"Force yourself to Eliminate, Clear out the Clutter and get Organized".

Shopping With

ESP

Essential Shopping Principles

So, how does one get organized? Well, I have a simple solution that is easy to follow to assist you with putting things in order. Let us start with your closet:

1. Examine and Evaluate

This may not be easy. You may find yourself doubting whether to keep a particular item or to let it go. You may make all sorts of excuses as to why you should hold on to something.

Your emotions and personal attachments will be very high as you go through this step. If you feel that you are not strong enough to do this alone ask a friend whom you trust to help you complete this task without emotion.

If you consider your spouse or significant other to be an unbiased and objective person, then ask them to help you with this task. If not, do not even take the risk of asking him/her to assist you. From my own experience, having their help will result into an unnecessary argument that you will want to avoid having.

To lessen the pain you may want to complete this step in phases; one month you will want to do your closets, the next month your drawers, followed by your jewelry and other accessories.

Shopping With

ESP

Essential Shopping Principles

2. Eliminate and Remove

Get rid of all those clothes, shoes and accessories you're not wearing anymore (especially, if you are holding on to them for sentimental reasons – or in hopes of getting back to your "high school" weight and size – even if you did – you probably wouldn't wear those clothes again). If you have not worn them in the past 2 years, you are not likely to wear them again.

The very first time you complete the step you should have a mass removal of all those items that have been taking up space and collecting dust for years. You will find yourself asking why you held on to all those things for so long.

3. Clear out the clutter and get organized

One of the reasons we shop is because we tell ourselves that we have nothing to wear; when in fact we have plenty; we just do not know what we have or where it is. So after you have examined and evaluated; eliminated and removed, you will want to; clear out the clutter and get organized by doing the following:

- Put order into your closet; suits, pants, dresses and blouses, etc. Place these items in an organized fashion in full view (if at all possible) so that you know what you "have and don't have" and you do not end up with duplicates of the same item.

Notice I said same items not same color. I will be the first to admit that I do have some duplicate blouses in my closet, but it is not because I made a duplicate purchase – they were gift items that I just decided to keep.

- **Shoes, Hats, Handbags, Belts and Scarves** – These items may be a little more difficult to place in your closet in plain view (depending on your closet size). For me, I have most of my shoes in clear plastic boxes on shelves inside my closet.

Whenever possible I throw away my shoeboxes. Ladies – your designer shoes will still look good on your feet without their boxes so do not concern yourself with keeping the boxes.

In my closet, I also have space to store my hats (on shelves or in hatboxes) and a place to hang my belts and store my sweaters and scarves.

Shopping With ESP *Essential Shopping Principles*

Years ago, I invested in having closet organizers installed in my walk-in closet and it was one of the better decisions I have made. Therefore, I would recommend that you consider doing this as well.

The biggest advantage to having the organizers installed is that it give you the ability to quickly scan your closet (to take an inventory of your belongings) and stay well organized. As mentioned earlier --when you go shopping you will have the ability to have a mental picture of what you already have so that you can accessorize or eliminate the risk of buying something you do not really need.

- **Drawers — under garments, nylons, socks, PJs, and night garments**, (by now you should have a picture in your mind of how this looks today and how you want it to look starting tomorrow).

I like to be able to open my drawers and see that my under garments are organized. I like my socks in a separate drawer, as well as my lingerie. I realize that organization is a matter of preference so I will not dwell on this; except to say that you will want.

- **Finally, that overly cluttered Jewelry Box** – How many of you have your fashion jewelry in a shoebox, plastic bin, basket or just lying on top of your dresser? I hate to ask, but I am sure there are those of you who may even have your fine jewelry mixed-in with your fashion pieces.

Well guess what?

Your jewelry needs organizing too. If you choose to store your fashion jewelry in a box or plastic bin – consider separating the necklaces from the earrings, brooches, and bracelets.

In the process of organizing, you will want to eliminate those pieces that are worn and the ones that you have not bothered to wear in two or more years. Yes – eliminate.

All they are doing is taking up space and adding clutter to your closets or drawers. Again, if you believe that you cannot be unbiased about what to keep or throw away then bring in a neutral party (someone who will have the ability to remove items without giving it a second thought).

Shopping With

ESP

Essential Shopping Principles

Getting organized will take time and I realize how terribly difficult this principle will be to master. Nevertheless, once you are organized, and go shopping, you will do so with a purpose and a mission.

You will see how much easier it will be to find something that compliments what you already have. You will quickly realize that you will be able to shop for what you more often need than shop for what you want.

Again, I cannot stress this enough, but over time, you will learn that you no longer need or want some of the items you have previously purchased (through impulse shopping) or have never worn and you will be strong enough to:

Let them Go!

Shopping With

ESP

Essential Shopping Principles

When you are in the process of eliminating items from your closet or drawers, you may want to consider:
Trading or swapping, donating, consigning or selling them on the internet (sites like eBay or ioffer).

The following illustrations are examples of how you might want to organize your clothing and accessories.

Sweaters, Knit Sweaters, Knit Pants, Wool Scarves and Hats

Shopping With

Essential Shopping Principles

Casual Wear

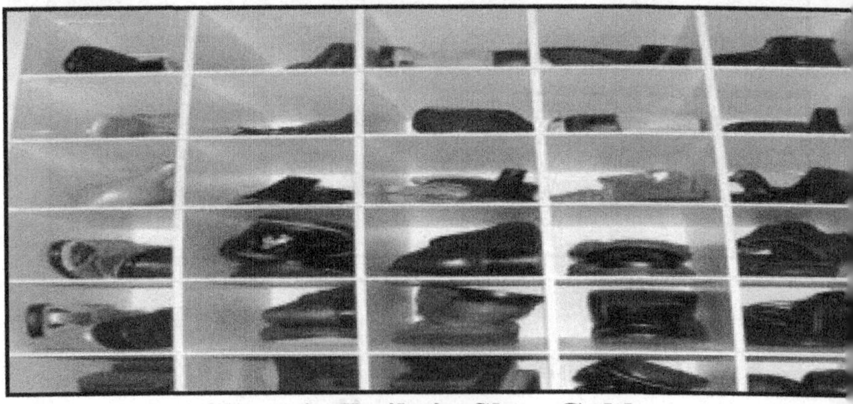

Shoes in Built-in Shoe Cubby

Shopping With

ESP

Essential Shopping Principles

Shoes in Plastic Shoe Boxes

Short Skirts and Blouses

Shopping With

Essential Shopping Principles

Jackets, Long Sleeve Blouses and Suits

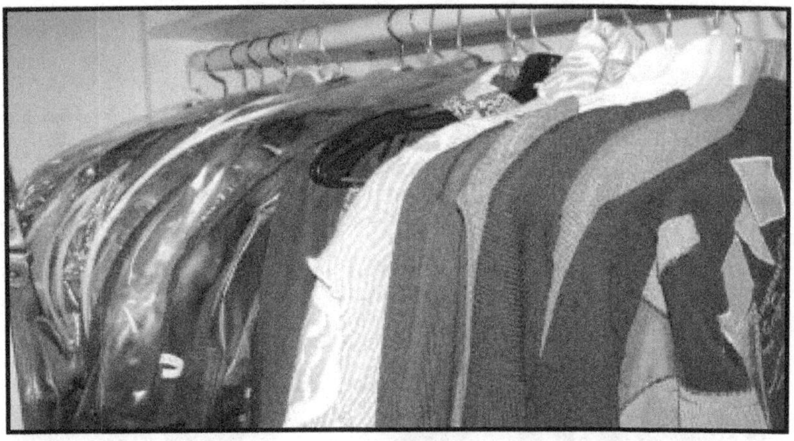

Knits and Wool (Dresses, Pants Suits)

Shopping With

Essential Shopping Principles

Slacks, Skirts and Dresses

Sweater Jackets and Long Sleeve Cotton Tops & Sweaters

Shopping With

ESP

Essential Shopping Principles

Casual Blouses

Silk Blouses

Shopping With

Essential Shopping Principles

Hats

Tops is a Built-Closet Drawer

Shopping With

Essential Shopping Principles

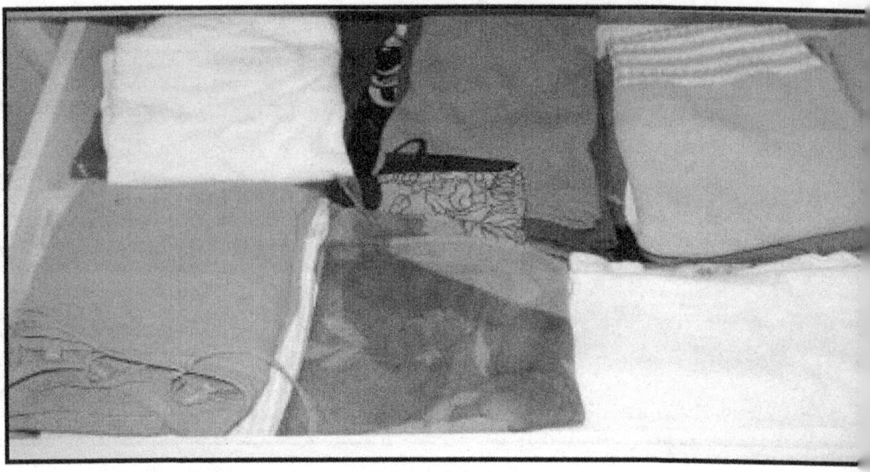

Camisoles and Sleeveless Tops

Purses on a Shelf

Hats and Hat Boxes

I hope that this has given you some ideas as to how you might organize your closet. Try it out and share your experience and results with your friends.

By the way, this a great exercise for both males and females. I would also recommend that if you have children – teach them to organize their belongings now (toys, clothes and books). Who knows they may come back and thank you for teaching them how to organize and be clutter free when they are older and living in their own homes. This is a wish for you.

Shopping With

Essential Shopping Principles

Shopping Principle Four
"Shop with Patience"

Growing up in the city of Philadelphia in the sixties had its' advantages; I really loved going "downtown" with my mother and aunts (who so loved to shop as well as to "Window Shop"). Shopping in the city is still so much fun. Shopping in city in the outdoors instead of being inside in a mall is exciting and alive.

Stores like Gimbles, Lit Brothers, and Strawbridge & Clothiers, John Wanamaker's, Lord and Taylors, Bakers Shoe Store, dress shops and hat stores always had great window displays.

One of the most memorable outings for me were the ones where we (my mom, aunts, and me) would just go out and "look" at what was in the store window displays and inside the stores on the racks. The John Wannamaker's Department Store Christmas tree inside their store was a must see every year.

Shopping With

Essential Shopping Principles

I also enjoyed listening to the conversations my mom and aunts would have about the price of a particular item and then say –

"Let's wait on this one and buy it when it goes on sale"
Sometimes their conversations would be about looking in a store catalogue to see if the prices were the same or to see if the items could be placed on "layaway"; before, there were credit cards – "lay-a-way" was a great option and just about every store offered this option to their shoppers.

So you see, at an early age I was exposed to "shopping with patience" and exploring options like the store catalogues. Today we now have the option of looking online to compare prices before making a purchase.

Living in the city provided me with several venues at which we could shop. We had specialty stores back then like the millinery stores, shoes stores, hosiery stores, specialty dress shops and lingerie stores as well as the big department stores mentioned.

Across the bridge from Philadelphia is New Jersey where we would shop at Loehmann's and there is New York City just a few hours away by train or car. We would also go to New York and shop on Sundays on Delancy Street with my aunts.

I remember my mother and other women in the neighborhood going on bus trips to Reading Pennsylvania and Burlington New Jersey to the outlets. They would make these trips once a year and my mother would take her money that she had set aside just for these special outings.

When I think back on my childhood and my young adult, experiences I realize why I still love and enjoy shopping to this day.

Preparing to shop patiently will be awkward and might even be uncomfortable at first. It takes:

- Time,
- Patience and a
- Willingness to Change.

Once you have mastered this shopping mindset, it will become second nature for you to

"Shop with Patience"

Shopping With

ESP

Essential Shopping Principles

"You don't need to have a reason to go shopping -- but you should always have a reason to spend your money".

I believe that "**Shopping" and "Spending"** are two very distinct and different activities. They are not the same, so do not be confused.

I am a person who can shop almost every day and at times for hours (as many as 4 hours or more in a given day) and return home most times empty-handed.

You may be asking yourself, -- "How is this possible"? Well, the fact of the matter is --- I am waiting for the – **"Right Price"**

I define The "Right Price" as the dollar amount that "I" am willing to pay. Therefore, this will vary for each person since we all have a different tolerance or threshold level that we have set for ourselves. I believe this is true even for people who are wealthy.

Shopping With

ESP

Essential Shopping Principles

Since I shop almost every day, I am able to catch merchandise as it comes into the store and take advantage of a sale that may or may not be advertised. Shopping every day also has its advantages --- the retailers and shop owners get to know you and your preferences in merchandise, and will often look out for those items.

They will set aside these items and call you. You become a preferred customer without having to sign in a guest book, sign-up for a credit card or even make a purchase; or feel guilty for not doing so.

Those of you who shop for the moment are usually shopping for the "Ready to wear" outfit or got to have it "ASAP".

Be honest --- how many times have you gone to the store -- made your purchase – and worn the outfit or shoes out of the store on your way to your event?

Okay, this may sound ridiculous, but if this sounds familiar – then this is not ridiculous to you.

Shopping With

ESP

Essential Shopping Principles

"Shopping With Patience" requires a certain mindset and discipline. In addition, there is the essential component of "time-management". Yes, time management.

It is my belief that the better you become at managing your time the smarter you will become at shopping.

So, I guess you are asking yourself -- how does this work? Well, here is an exercise you may want to consider doing to understand this concept.

Over the next three months set aside 5 - 7 hours a week, which you dedicate to nothing else except to shop. Notice I said "shop" which does not mean that you have to spend money each time you shop. This exercise will allow you to go out, explore, and test your patience.

Before you go out, map out your time for shopping. Identify what stores you will go to or how much time you will spend on the internet. You do not have to have a particular item in mind every time, but it will help if you have some idea of what you think you will need.

Shopping With

ESP

Essential Shopping Principles

Each time you do this, you will want to also exercise the Validity Check Test and create a mental picture of what you already own. You will also want to make sure that you avoid the following:

1. **Impulse buying** – making a purchase based solely on want rather than need

2. **Pressure from sales persons and friends** – only you can say what you need – be empowered and take control

3. **Pity Party** – The “woe is me” shopping spree

4. **Spend because you have extra money** – There’s nothing wrong with deciding to bank or invest this money instead of spending it on something you don’t need

Shopping With

ESP

Essential Shopping Principles

When you can do these things successfully (every time you go shopping) – then you are able to ---"Shop with Patience".

You are probably wondering if it is possible to achieve this principle. My answer to you is this – absolutely!

Smart Shoppers Exercise Patience

Shopping With

Essential Shopping Principles

Shopping Principle Five
"Window Shop"

Window Shopping is not a new concept, but for some it is the hardest thing to do… Why, you ask? Well, because there are some people who just cannot resist the temptation to make a purchase instead of just looking and admiring what they see.

I especially like to window shop as a way to see what the latest trend in fashion and accessories are as well as to get out into the mix of shoppers.

Window displays are a very important tool used to capture the shoppers' interest and to entice them to come into the store and hopefully make a purchase.

When my mother and aunts would go window-shopping they would make it very clear to each other that they were not to spend any money (after all the sole purpose of their outing was to just window shop). They were so committed and always stayed true to the idea of just window-shopping.

Shopping With

FSP

Essential Shopping Principles

When I reflect on those shopping trips it is easy for me to understand how I can go shopping and return home empty handed. That experience has made such a profound impact on my life and has greatly influenced my shopping attitude and behavior.

It is funny because at times when I do go shopping with my girlfriends they cannot understand why I do not find anything that I want to buy and they can manage to find things to buy.

Well, the truth is, I have already been window shopping, already made a purchase earlier, or I am waiting patiently for the "right price" for something I want to buy.
Since I window shop often it is not a problem for me to go shopping with my friends. You too will enjoy the experience of window-shopping once you can do it with confidence and the understanding that you do not have to make a purchase.

If you are not familiar with window-shopping, do not worry if you are not successful the first time you attempt this principle (especially if you are a shopaholic).

Shopping With ESP *Essential Shopping Principles*

I would recommend that you bring along a friend who is more disciplined than you are and let him/her know that you only want to look, admire, fondle and leave without making a purchase.

This person must have a strong will and be able to insist that you hold true to the idea of window-shopping.

Do not bring along someone who will let you get away with doing what you want and not being committed to the intended purpose of the outing (window-shopping).

Window dressings were much more elaborate once upon a time, especially during the holidays. Merchants would really go all out with their window displays. My opinion is that mall windows just do not compare to those of the past. The holiday window displays were a big part of my nostalgia that I will always remember.

Today, merchants still use window displays to attach shoppers into their stores. The intent is to get you in the store and for you to walk out the store with a purchase in hand.
So, when this happens, the merchants' window display has proven to be effective.

Shopping With

Essential Shopping Principles

My wish for you is that you will acquire a fondness for window-shopping and eventually reap the benefits of spending your money wisely and being empowered to do so.

So many ways that you can window shop were not available in the past. Technology has made it possible for you to window shop from almost anywhere. The internet gives us this luxury, but it does not allow you to fondle the item as you would if you were in the store.

I enjoy surfing the internet, looking at fashion magazines and window-shopping as a means of shopping with knowledge.

I am one who loves to find a bargain. It is great when I can find what I want for as little money as possible.

Oftentimes I am able to find authentic designer labels for less than the designer prices. I am so thrilled when this happens. I feel very much empowered and in control of how my money was spent.

Once you adapt and apply this shopping principle to your shopping habit, you too will enjoy the experience and become the master of your shopping and spending habits.

Shopping With
ESP
Essential Shopping Principles

Try keeping track of every time you go out to just window shop by journaling about your experience.

After the event, document the experience and capture the following:

1. How did you window shop (by going out or by surfing the internet)?

2. Where did you go?

3. Describe what you looked for.

4. How did this experience make you feel?

5. What action did you eventually take?

You will quickly learn that principle requires discipline and patience to master; however once you have mastered it, I believe it will become an essential part of your shopping experience forever.

Shopping With
ESP
Essential Shopping Principles

Like all the other principles in this book, this may also seem too simple. Nevertheless, it is much easier to tell you how to follow these principles than it will be for you to master them.

It will be especially hard if you are one who cannot resist the temptation or the urge to buy something just because you are in the store.

You may want to experiment with this principle by going to the store and leaving your credit cards at home and taking just enough money to purchase gas and a meal.

I know that some department stores will allow you to show your driver's license to look up your account – but do not do this, either.

If you go to the mall you will want to go from store to store looking, admiring and fondling the items that you like or think you might want to purchase later (place these items on your watch list).

Shopping With
ESP
Essential Shopping Principles

When window-shopping at a store like Marshall's; you may want to get a shopping cart. If you do, then place your purse inside the cart and walk around the store like you would do at the Mall store.

If you feel you must, you can place items in your shopping cart. However, remember, you are not to make a purchase you are just window-shopping.

Only place those items that you are seriously thinking about buying in the cart. Also, have a mental picture of what you already have as well to assess whether you want or need the items. Then place them on your watch list.

When you place something on your watch list you should be checking other stores, catalogues and the internet to see if the item can be purchased for less or at your "right.

Window shopping is a lot of fun and you can spend countless hours going from store to store, surfing the internet and looking through catalogues without spending a single penny (until you want to).

Shopping With

ESP

Essential Shopping Principles

You're the one with the power to decide when and how you'll spend your money $$$

Shopping With

ESP

Essential Shopping Principles

Shopping Principle Six

"Purchase What you Need First and What you Want Last"

How many times have you gone shopping just because? Then, when you get to the store, you see something and you say to yourself that you just have to have it?

This has happened to almost all of us and on many occasions, we end up purchasing something that we do not really need.

The proof of this may be the fact that the item or items purchased end up adding more clutter to the already existing clutter that you already created.

If you have successfully eliminated the clutter and gotten organized you should not have any problem with this principle.

Your shopping radar and lens should be able to conjure up a mental picture of what you already have and you will be able to compliment anything from clothing, furniture, linens, etc...

Shopping With

Essential Shopping Principles

You'll be completely amazed at how well you'll be able to compliment an existing outfit with coordinating accessories; for example, turning a pair of pants that you own into a three piece suit complete with accessories by simply adding a blazer, blouse, matching hat, watch, shoes or boots.

The fun thing about this is that you may be lucky (as I seem to be) and can find the same clothing label for the coordinated items as the one you have on the pants you own (that were purchased a year or two ago). This is one of the very reasons I like to shop at consignment stores.

People often ask me how I am able to find hats and purses that match so perfectly with the outfits that I wear. They want to know if I made the purchases together and if the outfits and matching accessories were displayed that way.

Since I have organized my closets — it makes it so easy for me to see something and know what will compliment what I already have.

Shopping With

Essential Shopping Principles

When I shop for a new outfit, it does not matter to me if I purchase the outfit before purchasing the shoes. When I see a pair of shoes that I absolutely love, I determine if I already have an outfit to compliment them. If not, I will buy them and then set out to find the right outfit to go with them.

Anyone who really knows me will tell you that I am a person who loves hats, shoes, and accessories (purses, watches, jewelry, and scarves). In my opinion, these accessories just complete an outfit to a tee. I guess I am a bit nostalgic and a traditional east coaster in that respect.

However, even before I decide to make a purchase I make sure that I check myself by doing the Validity Check Test (is this a need or is this a want?).

Shopping With

ESP

Essential Shopping Principles

You must clearly understand that there is a major distinction between a need and a want. The distinction for me is whether you are making the purchase out of necessity or "just because". You really do not need anything, but you just want it for immediate gratification or some other reason. It is this thinking and behavior; you will want to eliminate by keeping principle #6 in your shopping routine.

Now, I know there will be occasions when you are out shopping with friends and you will be tempted to spend money. However, if you practice the Validity Check Test and have a mental picture of what you have in your closet, even shopping with your friends will be enjoyable.

You will become so empowered by this new way of shopping, especially knowing that you are really purchasing what you need.

Your friends should notice this unusual behavior and the change in the way you shop to the point that they will inquire about what it is you are doing differently.

Shopping With

ESP

Essential Shopping Principles

Share with them this principle and if you are out shopping, demonstrate the Validity Check Test exercise (is this a "want or need?") with them.

You may not want to go as far as the mental picture, since they have probably not read this book and may not understand this practice. If they seem interested and want to know more about your shopping behavior—then — tell them to purchase this book.

Fondling the clothes and taking the Validity Check Test with a Friend

Shopping With

ESP

Essential Shopping Principles

Shopping Principle Seven
"Enjoy Yourself and have Fun"

I absolutely love to shop and to shop with family and close friends. There are those who may say that I am a "Shopaholic" but then they have no clue about my shopping behavior and shopping principles.

My reason for writing this book is to share with close friends and others my views and experiences that I believe have really allowed me to enjoy shopping in the manner that I do.

I really enjoy going shopping and having fun in the process. The best thing that I can offer those of you who "shop and hide" is this book. When you "shop and hide", I do not believe you can really have an enjoyable shopping experience.

People who practice the shop and hide behavior tend to be more focused on how they will get their purchases into the house without someone discovering that they have gone shopping and spent money. They may also begin to feel guilty and then return their purchases the next day or weeks later.

Shopping With
ESP
Essential Shopping Principles

You'll want to shop without guilt and stress so that you feel like you are in control and that you are truly empowered in a way that puts a smile on your face every time you have a shopping experience.

Once you are empowered, one of the things that I truly hope that you will be able to experience is that you do not overreact to those signs and ads announcing a sale or clearance. Even the going out of business, everything most go is not that great a deal or savings.

If you are window-shopping often, you will realize the timing and frequency of store markdowns; discover alternative shopping options (consignment stores, trading things and the internet) and focus more on getting what you need at the "right price".

If you any way like most shoppers, you enjoy finding that "needle in the haystack" or that unannounced sale.

By shopping often and using alternative shopping options (beyond the brick and mortar stores), you may also be very successful in finding exactly what you need in that haystack.

Shopping With
ESP
Essential Shopping Principles

First, always know what you need. Then set out on your shopping journey to find it. For example, when you are shopping for clothing or accessories (this item can be a particular couture label or simply an unknown designer or store brand label) go to your favorite consignment or retail store. Tell the owner or salesperson exactly what you looking for and if it is not in the store then I ask the owner or salesperson to call you if it comes into their store.

Your journey does not have to stop there. Try surfing the internet and looking through catalogues searching for what you need.

This might take quite some time before you actually get what you need, but it will be well worth it once, you find what you were searching for and need.

You may have to shop for weeks but in the process, you are becoming very empowered by staying focused on the goal (getting what you need).

I am not saying that you do not make a purchased (until you find what you are looking for). While searching for a particular item you may find something, you had not planned on buying, but need as well.

Shopping With

Essential Shopping Principles

After completing the Validity Check Test and seeing your mental picture of what you have — you decide to make the purchase.

By now, you should have some idea that shopping using these seven principles is an iterative process that improves and gets better each time you have a shopping experience.

Becoming an empowered shopper begins at principle one **(Making an Attitude Adjustment)** and continues through principle seven (**Enjoy Yourself and Have Fun**) and repeats and improves continuously throughout your life.

Shopping With

ESP

Essential Shopping Principles

AFFIRMATION STATEMENT

Starting today, I will become an empowered shopper by using the Essential Shopping Principles each time I go shopping!

With ESP:

1. I am learning how to become an empowered individual; one who makes shopping and purchasing decisions based on knowledge (what I already own), information (research and price comparisons) and validity (want or need) rather than impulse.
2. I am learning the importance of being organized and how to manage my time so that I am not stressed, pressured, or rushed to make a purchase.
3. I am learning that shopping does not have to mean that I have to spend money.
4. I am learning to let go and to get rid of those things I no longer need.
5. I am learning to be a more discipline shopper.
6. I am learning to have fun and to enjoy my shopping (me time) without any guilt.

Shopping With

Essential Shopping Principles

Some of Pat's Favorite Online Shopping Sites

Ebay.com

This is a great site; if you are a smart shopper, you can easily get items below retail price or at the "right price" for you. This is a bidding site so do not get to competitive and lose control. Decide on your price and stick with that (even if you get out bid).

Ioffer.com

I especially like this site because in my opinion it has more flexibility. Not only do you get to bid, but you also get to give your own price upfront. You can negotiate with the seller on the prices of the item, shipping as well as multiple purchases.

Strawberrynet.com

If you are looking for a particular fragrance or cosmetic product that has been discontinued by your favorite store– you will want to try this site. Here you will find fragrances and other cosmetics at a very reasonable price.

Scentdirect.com

This is another one of my favorite sites for perfumes and cosmetics. Here too you will find those hard to find fragrances.

Shopping With

ESP

Essential Shopping Principles

Finally, I also like going directly to the web sites for some of my favorite designer labels, like COACH, SAK, Chico's, and Michael Kors. I check out the sale or clearance items first to see what is there and I am checking to see the latest designs being featured. Well, I hope that you have enjoyed reading this book as much as I have enjoyed writing it.

Remember change does not happen overnight, so it will take practice, patience, and time to undo those years of undisciplined shopping habits that you have acquired.

However, each time you shop and use ESP, you'll find shopping to be one with a purpose as well as an adventure.

What I really enjoy about my shopping philosophy and behavior is – exercising my power and knowledge to spend my money when I need to and having patience to wait and find exactly what I need for the price I am willing to pay.

Shopping With

ESP

Essential Shopping Principles

This is an awesome experience and one that I have enjoyed often, and so can you when you begin to shop with ESP!

By purchasing this book:

You Are on Your Way to becoming an organized, empowered and smart shopper!

Shopping With

ESP

Essential Shopping Principles

Empowered Shoppers have so much Fun!

About The Author

Patricia Lott is a business professional and educator with style and flare. She is the co-founder of a non-profit organization "Riches By Design, Money Matters Network, Incorporated" which is committed to cultivating and encouraging high scholastic standards for middle and high school students in the areas of math, reading and financial literacy. Patricia was born in Augusta Georgia and raised in Philadelphia Pennsylvania.

Patricia has always loved fashion and shopping. Her love of hats is her fashion trademark. Ask anyone about Pat (as she prefers to be called) and they will also mention those beautiful hats" and how well dressed she always is.

Pat is very passionate about how she presents herself. She enjoys looking good without having to spend a huge amount of money, which is utmost important for her.

Pat is her own fashion icon and has the unique quality of style, colors, and coordination. Pat believes that we should all be empowered and in total control of our finances. It is this belief that has inspired her to write this book to share her shopping principles so that you and your friends can enjoy shopping as much as she does "guilt free".

Learning to apply critical thinking, organization, money, and time management skills, which Pat believes are the foundational life skills that make for a rich and empowering life.

Made in the USA
Monee, IL
04 November 2026

67378666R00046